Orhan Veli

Orhan Veli

The Complete Poems

*Translated from Turkish,
edited, and introduced by*

George Messo

Shearsman Books

First published in the United Kingdom in 2016 by
Shearsman Books
50 Westons Hill Drive
Emersons Green
BRISTOL
BS16 7DF

Shearsman Books Ltd Registered Office
30–31 St. James Place, Mangotsfield, Bristol BS16 9JB
(*this address not for correspondence*)

www.shearsman.com

ISBN 978-1-84861-437-6

Copyright ©
Yapı Kredi Kultur Sanat Yayıncılık Ticaret ve Sanayi AŞ, 2003

Translations, Introduction and Notes copyright © George Messo, 2016
The right of George Messo to be identified as the translator of this work has been asserted by him in accordance with the
Copyrights, Designs and Patents Act of 1988.
All rights reserved.

ACKNOWLEDGEMENTS

The translator wishes to thank the editors of the following magazines, blogs and online sites where some of these translations first appeared:

Loch Raven Review: 'See what happens', 'Beautiful weather', 'For the motherland'; *Metamorphoses*: 'Exodus I', 'Exodus II'; *Bülent*: 'For Free', 'Days', 'For You', 'Toward Freedom'; George Messo's Blog: 'To Live.'

A special note of thanks to Dr. Şenol Bezci of Ankara University, who corrected earlier versions of these translations and made many valuable suggestions.

Contents

Orhan Veli: A Brief Life	10
A Chronology of Orhan Veli	16
Guide to Pronunciation	22

Part One: Collected Poems

Garip / Strange (1941)

Nearing Gemlik	25
Robinson Crusoe	26
Dream	27
People	28
Public holiday	29
Exodus I	30
Exodus II	31
My left hand	32
My shadow	33
My eyes	34
In the sticks	35
The cabby's wife	36
Gossip	37
Epitaph I	38
Epitaph II	39
Epitaph III	40
My trouble's different	41
?	42
Going to war	43
Headache	44
Until morning	45
For Istanbul	46
It's just great	47
Did I fall in love?	48
My boats	49
Beautiful weather	50
Topsy-turvy	51

Illusion	52
I can't explain	53
Cornelian cherry	54
My ex-wife	55
Birds tell lies	56
Festival	57
Kasida	58
It makes me blue	59
Gossip	60

VAZGEÇEMEDIĞIM / MY COMPULSION (1945)

This world…	63
Hero of a novel	64
Beard	65
Journey	66
Song of Istanbul	67
Sound of a train	68
Not that, no	69
About to leave	70
Keşan	71
Guest	72
I gather old things	73

DESTAN GIBI / LIKE AN EPIC (1946)

Songs of the road	77

YENISI / THE NEW ONE (1947)

Souvenir	85
My gold tooth	86
Something fishy	87
Poem with a club	88
In	89
Poem with tweezers	90
Poem with a dove	91
Oh! My long lost youth!	92
For those who long for the sea	93
The Covered Bazaar	94

Near death	95
Poem with bells	96
Poem with a flutter	97
Sprawled out	98
Altındağ	99

Karşı/ Up against it (1949)

Days	102
For you	104
I'm listening to Istanbul	105
Toward freedom	107
Galata bridge	108
Up against it	109
Mahmut the dreamweaver	110
The first days of Spring	111
Poem of loneliness	112
Separation	113
Inside	114
See what happens	115
For free	116
For the motherland	117
The Ahmets	118
Erol Güney's cat…	119
Flea verse	120

Part Two: Uncollected Poems
Published 1937–1950

Tree	125
Hoy lu-lu	126
Sea	127
Slope	128
Journey	129
Sunday evenings	130
Poems on asphalt	131
Edith Almera	132

My tree	133
Being miserable	134
Bar	135
Voyage	136
People	137
Poems on travel	138
Are you alive?	139
Morning	140
Suicide	141
Goldfinch	142
Letters to Oktay	143
Sabri the mechanic	144
The Sicilian fisherman	145
For something to do	146
My bed	147
The story of Ali Rıza and Ahmet	148
Barbecue	149
My chatter	150
Like us	151
Carnation	152
Bird and cloud	153
Quantitative	154
Walking in the street	155
I'm Orhan Veli	156
Hay Kay	158
The water carrier's song	159
Wave	160
Poem with a tail	162
Reply	163
Relief	164
Adventure	165
Suddenly	166
Mermaid	167

Published posthumously 1951–1967

Incoming Poem	171
Parade of love	172
Poem with a hole	175
Rubaiyat	176
To live	177
My beloved	178
Something like whiskey	179
Over it all	180
Outside the city	181
That's life	182
Renaissance	183
Butter	184
Gangster	185
Goodbye	186
Recreation	187
On mustard	188
Lady in a white cloak	189
Yob	190
Thank god	191
Flag	192
Masterpiece	194
Bebek suite	195
To leave a city	197
A tiny heart	198
Landscape	199
Pictures	200
Notes	202
About the translator	207

Orhan Veli: A Brief Life

Sometime in 1939 Orhan Veli was travelling in a car together with his best friend and fellow poet Melih Cevdet Anday. As they drove past Çubuk Barrage in Ankara Anday suddenly lost control of the wheel. Their car sped off the road and somersaulted down a steep embankment. While Anday walked away unscathed, Orhan Veli spent the next 20 days in a coma. He was lucky to be alive. But he seemed thereafter destined to live on the edge.

* * *

Orhan Veli Kanık was born in Istanbul, capital of the Ottoman Empire, in 1914. The son of a prominent musicologist and conductor, he was privately educated at Galatasaray Lycée where French was the dominant language of instruction. When his father was appointed chief conductor of the State Orchestra in the newly founded Turkish Republic the family moved to Ankara. It was at the Ankara High School for Boys that he met his best friends and fellow-poets Melih Cevdet Anday (1915-2002) and Oktay Rifat (1914-1988). Among their teachers were several leading poets, including Ahmet Hamdi Tanpınar (1901-1962). He attended Istanbul University in 1933 only to drop out several years later without graduating. On his return to Ankara he took up a civil service position with the Postal Administration where he stayed until 1942. He was then enlisted as a reserve officer in the Armed Forces until 1945 when he again returned to Ankara and joined the Translation Bureau of the Ministry of Public Education. He translated a prodigious number of works from French into Turkish, including plays by Molière, Jean Anouilh, and Jean-Paul Sartre, before his sudden resignation in 1947.

Orhan Veli began publishing poetry as a student in the 1930s. His early poems were accomplished formal lyrics, following strictly controlled use of stanzaic forms and demanding quantitative syllabic metres. Many of these poems appeared in the influential monthly literary magazine *Varlık* under the pseudonym Mehmet Ali Sel. Despite their many technical accomplishments, the poems were imitative and unoriginal. Though he continued for some time to use his old pseudonym, midway through the 1930s Orhan Veli reached a turning point. The poetry underwent a sudden, radical change. In September 1937 six new poems appeared in *Varlık*, among them this simple, seven-line poem 'Journey':

> I've no plan to travel.
> But if I had
> I'd come to Istanbul.
> What would you do
> When you saw me on the Bebek tram?
>
> Anyway, like I said
> I've no plan to travel!

Written only one month earlier in Ankara, the step into print was short but the revolt total. Gone were the forced rhymes, the strenuous metres, the intricate metaphors, the perplexing allusions. Purged of all forms of familiar prosody Orhan Veli's new poems were virtually unrecognizable as poetry.

From the opposite end of a century saturated with free-verse it is difficult to appreciate the impact these new poems had on audiences schooled in the long traditions of Ottoman verse. Like Nâzım Hikmet (1902-1963) before him, who was the first Turkish poet to explore the possibilities of free verse, Orhan Veli was viciously lampooned by the literary establishment of his day. In a typically melodramatic outburst one famous critic, Yusuf Ziya Ortaç (1895-1967) wrote:

> The insane asylum and the flop-house of art are now joined hand in hand... O Turkish Youth! I appeal to you to spit in the face of such shamefulness![i]

---

[i] Quoted in Halman, T.S. (1997) 'Introduction' in *Just For the Hell of It: Selected Poems of Orhan Veli Kanık* (İstanbul: Multilingual Yayınları).

From 1935 onward Orhan Veli became increasingly familiar with the experimental poetics of Dadaism and Surrealism. He was among the first Turkish poets to translate Jules Supervielle (1884-1960) and Philippe Soupault (1897-1990)[ii]. In the consciously underplayed rhetoric of Soupault's early poems from *Chansons* (1921) and *Georgia* (1926) Orhan Veli found a stylized naivety of arresting power and relevance.

In 1941 he published his first book, *Garip* (Strange), a collaborative anthology with poems by Melih Cevdet Anday and Oktay Rifat. The collection was prefaced with its own strident manifesto:

> 'The literary taste on which the new poetry will base itself is no longer the taste of a minority class… This does not signify that an attempt should be made to express the aspirations of the masses by means of the literary conventions of the past. The question is not to make a defence of class interests, but merely to explore the people's tastes, to determine them, and to make them reign supreme over art.' [iii]

While its iconoclasm consciously drew parallels with the French avant-garde, the attitude of the *Garip* poets was to turn even Surrealism on its head in poems which shocked the reader awake. Orhan Veli's colloquial spontaneity was already a matter of style, a crafted low-key anti-rhetoric coupled to a socially poignant anti-heroism. The *Garip* poets were masters of the 'artfully artless'.[iv] It was a poetry striking for its 'ordinariness and the aggressiveness of this ordinariness'.[v] And though they aligned themselves, in spirit, with the revolutionary aristocrat Nâzım Hikmet, their poetry spoke existentially, of real human

---

[ii] Orhan Veli met and interviewed Soupault in Kızılay, Ankara, in 1949 while Soupault was on a UNESCO visit to Turkey.

[iii] See Halman

[iv] Eagleton, T. (2007) *How to Read a Poem* (Oxford: Blackwell): p.9.

[v] Nemet-Nejat, M. (1989) 'Introduction' in *I, Orhan Veli*. (New York, NY: Hanging Loose Press).

experience in all its grubby, visceral splendour.

'We can arrive at a new appreciation by new ways and means. Squeezing certain theories into familiar old moulds cannot be a new artistic thrust forward. We must alter the whole structure from the foundation up.'[vi]

The book gave birth to the first truly modern wave in Turkish poetry, which came to be known as the *Garip Movement*. The neo-classical grandees they had begun by emulating, such as Yahya Kemal Beyatlı (1884-1958) and Ahmet Haşim (1884-1933), were now seen as the representatives of a regressive literary edifice, their poetry the outdated preserve of privileged elites:

'In order to rescue ourselves from the stifling effects of the literatures which have dictated our tastes and judgments for too many years, we must dump overboard everything that those literatures have taught us.' [vii]

And dump it they did. What they put in its place was poetry of unprecedented directness and simplicity. Its zen-like compression spoke of awakening and renewal. Over the decade that followed Orhan Veli grew into his role as the *enfant terrible* of Turkish letters, his lyric genius maturing in the longer, unforgettable poems from 1949, such as 'I'm Listening to Istanbul', 'For You', and 'Towards Freedom.'

* * *

Between 1941 and 1950 Orhan Veli published five short books: *Garip* (Strange, 1941), *Vazgeçemediğim* (My Compulsion, 1945), *Destan Gibi* (Like an Epic, 1946), *Yenisi* (The New One, 1947) and *Karşı* (Up Against It, 1949). The poetry retained its

---

[vi] See Halman
[vii] See Halman

power to provoke, in poems often no longer than a few flashing lines, such as 'For the Motherland':

> What didn't we do for this motherland!
> Some of us died;
> Some gave speeches.

He drew inspiration from his own domestic life, transforming the mundane facts of a peripatetic minor civil servant into some of the most memorable and often-quoted poems in the Turkish language. When he spoke of revolutionizing Turkish poetry, he could hardly have imagined the impact his writing would have. It is no exaggeration to say that Orhan Veli's influence, large or small, can be found in almost every aspect of modern Turkish poetry. His idiolect echoed the colloquial rhythms and vocabulary of the common man. His taste for controversy, together with his disdain for authority and artifice, earned the admiration of his friends and contemporaries, and invoked the wrath of the conservative establishment he railed against.

Orhan Veli's reputation was of mythic proportions and he was infamous for the womanizing and heavy drinking that fuelled a decade of creativity. But the booze eventually caught up with him. Following a prolonged binge on a weekend trip to Ankara he stumbled into an unmarked ditch and suffered what appeared to be minor head injuries. Several days later, on his return to Istanbul, he was rushed to hospital with acute head pains. Shortly afterwards he slipped into a coma and died. He was 36.

* * *

We can only guess what Orhan Veli might have done had he lived. Melih Cevdet Anday and Oktay Rifat enjoyed long writing lives, reinventing themselves several times over as poets, playwrights and novelists. If we trace through time any one of the many intricate paths that lead us to contemporary Turkish poetry, sooner or later we encounter Orhan Veli.

* * *

There have been many individual translations of Orhan Veli's poems into English. Two large book-length selections have also appeared in translation in the United States: Talat Halman's *I am Listening to Istanbul: Selected Poems of Orhan Veli Kanık* (1971) and Murat Nemet-Nejat's *I, Orhan Veli: Poems by Orhan Veli* (1989). Anyone familiar with these two remarkable books will recognise the extent to which their various resonances echo through the present volume. I acknowledge my immense debt to both these translators.

I make no attempt here to include any of Orhan Veli's early, formal lyric poems. The poet himself disowned them. What I have translated is the full output of his mature work, the poems for which he is best remembered and justly celebrated one hundred years after his birth.

A Chronology of Orhan Veli

Life	Historical / Cultural Background
1914 13 April: Orhan Veli born to Mehmet Veli Bey and Fatma Nigar Hanım in Yalıköyü, Istanbul, Ottoman Empire.	First World War. Turkey sides with Germany. 1915 French, British and Allied troops invade Gallipoli. 1918 Allies begin 4-year occupation of Constantinople. 1919 Greek army lands at Smyrna. Turks begin War of Independence.
1921 Orhan Veli enrolled at Galatasaray Public School as a boarder.	Ahmet Haşim, *Göl Saatleri*. 1922 Greek army defeated. Izmir (Smyrna) razed.
1923 Mehmet Veli Bey appointed conductor of Presidential Symphony Orchestra in Ankara. Also appointed professor at Ankara Conservatoire. Orhan Veli and his mother remain in Istanbul.	Declaration of the Turkish Republic. Mustafa Kemal becomes President. Capital moves to Ankara. 1924 Abolition of Islamic Caliphate.
1925 Orhan Veli moves with his mother to Ankara. Starts at Gazi School.	Abolition of the Fez. Western calendar adopted.
1926 Enrolled in Ankara High School for Boys where he meets Oktay Rifat	

Horozcu and Melih Cevdet Anday. Together they publish the poetry magazine *Sesimiz*. Taught by Ahmet Hamdi Tanpınar.

1932 Graduates from Ankara High School for Boys.

1933 President of Student Association. Enrols in Istanbul University Department of Literature.

1935 Drops out of university.

1936 Moves back to Ankara. Starts work for the State Postal Service. In the same year his early formal poems begin to appear in *Varlık* magazine under the pseudonym Mehmet Ali Sel.

1937 First appearance of new style poems. Oktay Rifat and Melih Cevdet also publish new free-verse poems.

1939 Involved in a car accident along with Melih Cevdet Anday. Spends 20 days in a coma.

1928 Language Reforms. Latin alphabet introduced.

Death of poet Ahmet Haşim.

1934 Women gain right to vote. Surname Law. Mustafa Kemal becomes Atatürk.

Nâzım Hikmet, *Taranta-Babu'ya Mektuplar*.

Sait Faik, *Semaver*.
Sabahattin Ali, *Kağnı*.
Nâzım Hikmet, *Şeyh Bedreddin Destanı*.

1938 Death of Mustafa Kemal Atatürk. Ismet İnönü becomes president. Nâzım Hikmet sentenced to 28 years' imprisonment.

1940 Fazıl Hüsnü Dağlarca, *Çocuk ve Allah*.

1941	*Garip* anthology published in May. Includes 24 poems by Veli, 16 by Anday, 21 by Rifat, with introduction by Veli.	
1942	Resigns from State Postal Service.	Asaf Hâlet Çelebi, *He*.
1942-5	Military service. Posted to Kavak, Gelibolu, as lieutenant.	
1945	Joins Ministry of Education, Ankara, translation department, specializing in French literature. February: publishes first solo collection, *Vazgeçemediğim*. April: second edition of *Garip*, with poems by Anday and Rifat removed.	Asaf Hâlet Çelebi, *Lâmelif*. Melih Cevdet Anday, *Rahatı Kaçan Ağaç*. Oktay Rifat, *Yaşayıp Ölmek*.
1946	Publishes *Destan Gibi*. Resigns from Ministry of Education.	
1947	Publishes *Yenisi*.	Edip Cansever, *İkindi Üstü*; İlhan Berk, *İstanbul*.
1948	Translates La Fontaine's *Fables*. Founds the bi-monthly magazine *Yaprak*, with Bedri Rahmi Eyuboğlu, Abidin Dino, Oktay Rifat and Melih Cevdet Anday.	Death of author Sabahattin Ali. Bedri Rahmi Eyuboğlu, *Karadut*.
1949	January: Issue 1 of *Yaprak*, includes Cahit	Ahmet Hamdi Tanpınar, *Huzur*.

Sıtkı Tarancı, Sait Faik Abasıyanık, and Fazıl Hüsnü Dağlarca. Joins three-day hunger strike for Nazım Hikmet's release from prison. Completes stories of Nasreddin Hoca. Publishes final collection of poems, *Karşı*. Translates Shakespeare's *Hamlet* and *The Merchant of Venice*.

1950 June: Final issue of *Yaprak*, number 28. Returns to Istanbul. 10 November: weekend trip to Ankara, suffers minor head injury after falling into a ditch. 14 November: back in Istanbul, suffers acute head pains and rushed to Cerrahpaşa Hospital. Diagnosed with cerebral bleeding and alcohol poisoning. Slips into a coma at 20.00 and dies at 23.20 same evening. 17 November: funeral service at Bayazit Mosque. Buried in Aşiyan Cemetery.

First democratic parliamentary elections. Democrat Party sweeps to victory. Adnan Menderes becomes prime minister. Nâzım Hikmet released from prison; flees to the Soviet Union.

1951 *Complete Poems*, Varlık Publishing.

Hikmet stripped of Turkish citizenship.

1953 *Prose Works*, Varlık.

1954 Death of Sait Faik.

2012 *Beni Bu Güzel Havalar Mahvetti*, Orhan Veli in his own voice. CD and Booklet, Yapı Kredi Publishers.

Part One

Collected Poems

A Guide to Pronunciation

With few exceptions, where Turkish appears in the book I have employed standard Turkish spelling. The exceptions are those words for which well established anglicized forms exist, such as *İstanbul* and *İzmir*, which are commonly written in English with *I* rather than *İ*.

As a guide to pronunciation the following may be useful:

a (*a* in *apple*)
b (as in English)
c (like *j* in *jam*)
ç (*ch* in *chips*)
d (as in English)
e (*e* in *pet*)
f (as in English)
g (*g* in *gate*)
ğ (lengthens a preceding vowel)
h (*h* in *have*)
ı (*i* in *cousin*)
i (*i* in *it*)
j (like *s* in *measure*)
k (*k* in *king*)
l (*l* in *list*)

m (as in English)
n (as in English)
o (*o* in the French *note*)
ö (as in German)
p (as in English)
r (*r* in *rug*)
s (s in sit)
ş (*sh* in *ship*)
t (as in English)
u (*u* in *put*)
ü (as in German)
v (as in English)
y (*y* in *yes*)
z (as in English)

Garip

Strange

(1945)

Nearing Gemlik
You'll see the sea.
Don't be surprised.

[*İnkilâpçı Gençlik*, 17.10.1942]

Robinson Crusoe

My gran is the most loved
Of all my childhood friends
Ever since we tried to save
Poor Robinson from his desert isle
And cried together
For wretched Gulliver's
Suffering
In the land of giants.

November 1937

[*Varlık*, 15.12.1937]

Dream

I saw my mother dead in a dream.
I woke up crying.
It reminded me of one holiday morning
Staring at the balloon I'd lost to the sky,
Crying.

1938

[*İnsan*, 1.10.1938]

People

How I love those people!
Those who look like others living
In the colourful, faceless world of decals
With chickens, rabbits and dogs.

Ankara, August 1937

[*Varlık*, 15.9.1937]

Public Holiday

Crows, be sure not to tell my mum!
When the cannon goes off today I'll leave
Home and sign up for the Ministry of War.
I'll buy you sweets, if you keep shut,
Simits and candy-floss too.
I'll let you into my swing-boat, crows,
I'll give you all of my marbles.
Come on crows, don't tell mum!

November 1938

[*Varlık*, 15.3.1940]

Exodus

I

From his window looking out on flat roofs
The harbour could be seen
And church bells
Rang endlessly all day.
Now and then,
And at night
Trains could be heard from his bed.
He began to fall in love with a girl
From the apartment opposite.
Even so
He left this city
And went to another.

Istanbul, November 1937

[*Varlık*, 15.12.1937]

Exodus

II

Now from his window
Poplars can be seen
Along the canal.
In the day it rains,
At night the moon comes out
And the square opposite becomes a market.
Be it a journey, money or a letter,
There's always something on his mind.

November, 1938

[*Garip I*, 1941]

My left hand

I got drunk
I thought of you again,
My left hand,
My clumsy hand,
My pitiful hand!

My shadow

I'm sick and tired of dragging it around,
For years, on the tips of my toes.
Let's live a little in this world,
My shadow alone,
Me by myself.

Ankara, September 1937

[*Varlık*, 15.12.1937]

My eyes

My eyes,
Where are my eyes?

The devil took them,
Carried them off,
Brought them back
Unsold.

My eyes,
Where are my eyes?

Istanbul, October 1937

[*Garip I*, 1941]

In the sticks

You're in the sticks,
Homesick like hell.
It's evening,
The sun goes down,
What the hell can you do but drink?

[*İnkılâpçı Gençlik*, 1.8.1942]

The cabby's wife

Lady, don't ruin me
Don't wave that way from your window
Undressing, shedding clothes
You've an eye on your brother-in-law
I've an eye on my youth
I'll not rot in prisons,
Don't make trouble for me,
Don't ruin me.

[İşte, 15.6.1944]

Gossip

Who was it
Said I was struck on Süheyla?
Who was it
Saw me kissing Eleni
Near Yüksek Kaldirim in broad daylight?
Then I grabbed Melahat
And took her to Alemdar, right?
I'll explain that later, but
Whose legs did I touch up on the tram?
Apparently I have a taste for Galata brothels,
Apparently we get smashed
And go there to unwind.
Don't waste your time,
Forget all that crap –
As if I don't know what I'm doing.

Or is it the story of me throwing Mualla
Into a rowboat and making her sing
"Your pain is in my heart"?

Epitaph

I

He suffered nothing in this world
More than he suffered from corns.
Although he was created ugly
He wasn't all that hurt.

He never took the Lord's name in vain
Unless his shoes pinched,
But he'd hardly count as a sinner.
It's a pity about Süleyman Efendi.

Ankara, April 1938

[*İnsan*, 1.10.1938]

Epitaph

II

For him "To be or not to be"
Wasn't a question at all.
One night he slept
And never woke up.
He was taken, carried away,
Washed, prayed for, and buried.
If his creditors hear of his death
They're sure to give up any claims.
And when his credit comes in...
Well, no one owed the deceased a thing.

January, 1940

[*Varlık*, 15.3.1940]

Epitaph

III

They put his rifle in the depot,
Gave his clothes to someone else.
Neither breadcrumbs in his satchel now
Nor lip prints on his can.
Such was the wind
That carried him away,
Not even his name was left.
Only this couplet remained
In his own hand on the coffeehouse wall:
"Death is God's command,
If only there was no parting."

September, 1941

[*İnsan*, 1943]

My trouble's different

Don't think it's the sun that bothers me;
So what if spring's here?
Or if the almond tree's in bloom?
We're not about to die.
Even if we are, should I be afraid
Of death that comes with the sun?
I'm one year younger every April,
Every spring I'm a little more in love.
Am I afraid?
Friend, my trouble's different…

?

Why when I say harbour
Do cranes come to mind
And sails when I say open sea?

Cats when I say March,
Workers when I say rights
And why does the old miller
Blindly believe in God?

And why does rain fall slanted
In windy weather?

Ankara, March 1938

[*İnsan*, 1.10.1938]

Going to war

Blonde haired child going to war!
Return as beautiful again.
The sea's scent on your lips
Salt on your lashes,
Blonde haired child going to war!

May, 1940

[*Garip I*, 1941]

Headache

I

No matter how beautiful the road,
No matter how cooling the night,
The body gets tired,
But the headache never dies.

II

Even if I go home now
I can leave again a little later,—
These clothes and shoes are mine
And the streets belong to no one.

Ankara, April 1938

[*İnsan*, 1.10.1938]

Until morning

Worse than lovers, these poets;
What suffering these men inflict;
Imagine, a whole night locked
In the inner rhyme of a poem?

Listen then, can you hear
The song of roofs and chimneys
Or ants carrying their grain loads
To their nests?

What if I didn't wait for sunset
To send those second-hand rhymes
To the coast
With dustmen who come to my door?

Satan implores: "Open your window;
And scream, scream, scream until morning."

April, 1939

[*Varlık*, 15.03.1940]

For Istanbul

April

It's impossible
To write poems
If you're in love,
And not to write
When April's the month.

Desires and Memories

Desires are different,
Memories different too.
Tell me, how can anyone live
In a city that doesn't see sun?

Insects

Don't think,
Just desire!
Look, that's what insects do.

Invitation

I'm waiting.
Come in the kind of weather
Where it's impossible to turn back.

April, 1940
[*Garip I*, 1941]

It's just great

It's just great, the colour of tea
Early morning
In the open air!
The weather's just great!
The young boy's just great!
The tea's just great!

[*Garip I*, 1941]

Did I fall in love?

Was I going to have these thoughts too,
Was I going to be sleepless like this,
To be silent and voiceless like this?
Never even to miss
My favourite salad?
Is that how I was going to be?

April, 1939

[*Varlık*, 15.3.1940]

My boats

In the pages of my picture book
My boats, my sailing boats.
Going to cannibal lands,
My boats, wind blown.
My boats, pencil drawn,
Red-flagged, my boats.
In the pages of my picture book
Leander's Tower,
My boats.

November 1938.

[*Varlık*, 15.3.1940]

Beautiful weather

This beautiful weather has ruined me,
It was in weather like this I quit
My job with the Office of Pious Foundations.
I got used to smoking in weather like this
And it was in just this weather I fell in love.
It was in weather like this I forgot
To take home bread and salt.
Always in this kind of weather
I relapse into my poetry-writing disease.
This beautiful weather has ruined me.

April, 1940

[*Garip I*, 1941]

Topsy-turvy

My arrow-struck heart,
On the shoe-shine's box,
My pigeon on wafers,
My sweetheart on the prow
Half fish
Half human
Am I a man?
Am I a jinn?
What am I?

Illusion

I'm saved from an old love,
Now all women are beautiful,
My shirt's new,
I've washed,
I've shaved,
It's peaceful.
Spring is here.
The sun is out.
I'm in the street, people are relaxed,
I'm relaxed too.

March, 1940

[*Ses*, 1.4.1940]

I can't explain

If I cry, do you hear me
In the lines of my verse
Can you touch my tears
With your hands?

Before I fell in with this sorrow
I never knew songs were so beautiful
And their words insufficient.

There's a place, I know,
Where you can say everything.
I feel I'm pretty close
But I can't explain.

April, 1940

[*Garip I*, 1941]

Cornelian Cherry

It gave its first fruit this year
Cornelian Cherry,
Three of them.
Next year it will give five.
Life is long,
We'll wait.
What can it matter?

Bless you, Cornelian Cherry!

April, 1940

My ex-wife

Do you know why it is
You're in my dreams every night?
Why it is Satan lulls me
Every night on snow white sheets,
Do you know why?
My ex-wife, I still love you.

You know, you're one hell of a woman!

Birds tell lies

Don't, my coat, believe
What the birds say,
You're my only confidante.

Don't believe it; every spring
The birds tell this same lie.
Don't, my coat, don't believe them.

April 1940

[*Garip I*, 1941]

Festival

The bread ration's done
And the coal supply's dusted.
Think no more about poverty,
Think no more of the house you'll build.
There's strength in the hand
And long enough yet to live.
God has an eye on the future,
So hold on my crazy heart!

Kasida

A Bursa blade in her hand,
A red scarf around her neck.
You whittle sticks all day
In Filya field.

For you I'm digging under walls,
You're climbing over them.

September 1940

[*Garip*, 1941]

It makes me blue

It makes me blue getting a letter,
Makes me blue drinking gin,
Makes me blue setting out on a trip.
I've no idea what will come of it.
When they sing the folk song "My Kâzım"
In Üsküdar
It makes me blue.

September, 1940

[*Garip I*, 1941]

Gossip

You're one kind of beauty in mirrors,
Another in bed.
Forget what they say,
Get dressed,
Put on your face,
Come down
Into the street
And spite them.

People will talk,
So let them.
Aren't you my lover?

February, 1941

[*Garip I*, 1941]

Vazgeçemediğim

My compulsion

(1945)

This world will drive you mad;
This night, these stars, this scent,
This tree in blossom from tip to root

Hero of a novel

Rain fell on my tent
Wind blew in the Bay of Saros
And I, hero of a novel
In my straw bed
In World War II
Burning oil at my bedstead,
Tried to live out my life
That began in a city
And will end who knows where
Who knows when.

[*Ülkü*, 1.1.1945]

Beard

Which of you can make lanterns
From pumpkins like me;
Or carve an old boat on them
With a pearl-handled knife;
Write poems
Or letters;
Sleep
Or get up;
Which of you can please
His girl
The way I do?

This beard didn't grey for nothing!

July, 1941

[*İnkilâpçı Gençlik*, 18.7.1942]

Journey

To Rıfkı Melûl Meriç

What is it about travelling
That always makes me cry,
Me, alone in this world?
One rosy dawn
I set off from Uzunköprü;
Trussed horses clipperty-clop
Their diver, a fourteen year old,
A sweet girl brushed me, knee to knee,
Head scarfed but bubbly;
My spirits should be high, right?
I wish!
Tell me, what's it about travelling?

Song of Istanbul

In Istanbul, on the Bosphorus,
I'm poor Orhan Veli,
Son of Veli,
Steeped in misery.

I'm sitting near Rumeli Hisar,
Sitting and singing a song:

"Istanbul's marble stones
Are landing on my head, landing oh, like seagulls,
My grieving tears pour out,
        My burden
        All because of you."

"The cinema's at the heart of Istanbul,
But mother needn't know how weird, how sad I am;
Others will talk, and make love. So what?
        Sweetheart,
        My flaws are down to you!"

In Istanbul, on the Bosphorus,
I'm poor Orhan Veli,
Son of Veli,
Steeped in misery.

[*Ülke*, 1.2.1945]

Sound of a train

I'm an outsider;
No beautiful girl to lift my heart
In this city,
Not even a familiar face;
When I hear the sound of a train,
My eyes
Are streaming.

Not that, no.

How can I tell you
How, how, about my trouble?
A terrible heartache,
Trouble my enemy should have.
About a broken heart, say…
Not that, no!
About money, say…
No, not that!
But trouble…

Impossible to bear.

About to leave

We gave up on material things,
Happy with our share of daylight.
We gave up on happiness,
Happy with our hope alone.
And finding neither of these
We invented miseries of our own.
But we couldn't be consoled.
Was it that we...
We were not of this world?

[*Ülkü*, 1.1.1945]

Keşan

21.8.1942,
In Republic Mall,
What a great night!
It rained as morning broke.

Sunrise, blood-speckled,
My soup came steaming hot,
And the truck came right to our door.

My stomach's packed,
Clothes on my back,
Edirne, here I come.

Guest

Bored rigid from dawn to dusk,
I chewed through two packs of cigarettes.
I wrote but nothing stuck.
I played the fiddle for the first time ever,
Walked around,
Watched the backgammon players.
I sang a song out of key,
I caught flies, a matchbox full.
God damn it, finally,
I got up and came here.

I gather old things

I gather old things,
Gather and make them into stars.
If music is the manna of love,
I just love music.

I write poems.
I write poems and gather old things,
Swapping old things for music.

I wish I were a fish in a bottle of gin.

Destan gibi

Like an epic

(1946)

Songs of the road

"I set out from Hereke,
Greetings left and right,
Hurry, my lonesome poet.
Safe journey!"

İzmit's streets were covered in leaves,
Skyward the city's unforgettable air,
Its songs on my lips,
My hands in pockets,
Going here, going there.
Autumn,
İzmit's streets were covered in leaves.

"İzmit's bridge is concrete through and through,
How ignorant are those who lay with you.
It's you I miss each day and each night too.
    My heart is scorched, my chest is torn apart,
    Oh, sweet sickness eats away my heart."

Arifiye!
The driver stopped and said this is the Institute.
The headmaster's name was Süleyman Edip.
Let's come to a halt here too.
With wart-pocked hands, a wand of light on their faces,
Let's raise a cheer
To those who walk with hope for tomorrow.

"The road to Ada is ankle deep
In chestnuts falling to my feet…"

Ada? I mean Adapazarı
Where glasses pass for bottles;
You're already brooding in your cups,
So sweetie, watch your step.

"Before the Government office I passed,
Drank coffee in my usual place,
Then saw, in Hendek, a beautiful face
And knew, my love, we'd never last;
    Stony are the Hendek lanes
    As lust for you tears through my veins."

Early, you're woken for a journey
Toward the rising sun,
Your troubles slowly fading now
At peace with the home you crave,
Focused on the work ahead.

"The road to Düzce straight as a die,
A beautiful young girl goes by."

I'm in Düzce, in the Yeşil Yurt Hotel.
There's a shop out front
And a bloke selling sâlep.

Through another sorrowful night I pass
With ballads and songs:

"Colours of their house all topsy-turvy,
The jilted lover knows so little mercy,
There must be even worse, I dare say."

Won't I get used to it,
Won't I be able to forget?
I slept after the sun went down
And got up before it rose.
I took a quick look out of the window:
The horizon was turning green.
I said, my sweetheart is now
In the fourth stage of her sleep,
Galata Bridge is about to be opened,

Dirty daylight is about to be poured
Into the ash coloured water.
Row boats, barges and skiffs
Jostle between waiting ships in port
As people muddle through their lives;
Men, women, and children
With lunch boxes in their hands,
Working girls going to Regie.

"Greetings from me to the governor of Bolu,
First climb the mountains you lean upon.
The mountains should echo and throng,
From fizzing arrows to the shield's hullabaloo."

Hey, hey!
Hey mountains, hey mountains, mountains of Bolu, hey!
Governors of Bolu, move aside, I'm on my way!
That's how it is, the wind from high places,
That's how it makes people talk.

Spiralling up, up the steep hill,
A whirling Dervish spins out;
Hanoğlu Kocabey appears
From behind İsa Balı;
Then Ayvaz, then Hoylu,
And Koroğlu from a precipice:
"With Mevlâ on my side I make it through,
You're my back, my fortress, hey mountains!"
Will the shoes withstand the marbled horse?
Mountains wake from their sleep
Earth and sky are splashed blood red.
If you've never passed through here,
Never drank this mountain dew,
Then you can't say you've ever lived, my friend.
This spring's too much for hands, for teeth,
And the cypress trees lay down.
From one of the carts bringing logs
A delicate voice floats up:

"Carts unload their heavy stocks
As the driver whips his docile ox,
Can't breath in, your head in a spin."

Wouldn't he spare his own ox?
All he has is a pair of bulls,
A daughter fit to wed,
Three small lambs;
Everything is so damned dear.

With a postman we exchanged a glance.
Dear postie, precious mailman,
Greetings to all my friends.

The city folk proclaim to the province,
Set up their radio in the council square;
A snippet of news we gave…
So bla bla bla…
We got petrol on the black market,
"Hang on!" we said.

The road to Gerede,
Reşadiye Lake.
A lake that…
Makes you want to be a poet and write poems.

"Evening time, once more my thoughts adrift"
I sat up on the ridge,
Thought back to the past.
I was a soldier then, back in Adilhan village;
It was a night like this,
The same yearning for Istanbul,
Wrapped in thoughts:

"These peaks aren't Koru's peaks,
These streets aren't Adilhan's streets,
That mill isn't Master Ferhat's,

Nor is this one of those miserable songs;
I don't hunger, nor do I thirst
Nor am I off on my own.
If only the sun would go down,

I'll take myself off to a bar tonight,
Put away a few glasses there.
The ferry still comes to its pier, anyway,
From across the Golden Horn.
Let its passengers pour out,
It's the best time to be in Eyüp now."

Come on sweetheart, let's hit the road.

Finally İbrıcık appeared.
Salam aleykum, grocer.
Aleykum salam, my boy.
We have a patient, waiting for a machine.
So, they have a patient waiting for a machine.

The coffeehouse seats reek of dung.
Everyone's trouble is different.
Where are you from?
Sinop.

"Oh, what trouble, Lordy Lord,
This life for my wretched destiny,
One lover follows another, O Lord,
Like a hell fire all over me."

"Gerede we reached on a Sunday,
Hookers in every alleyway,
When will this homesickness end, just say!
    My heart is scorched, my chest torn apart,
    Oh, sweet sickness eats away my heart."

We're on the Zonguldak road.
From the mountain tops
Suddenly we'll see the sea.
We'll see where the sea and sky meet.
We'll kiss with the northern wind.
He's a traveller and so are we,
The north wind will blow from far away.
On a sun drenched day
We'll see the Black Sea deepest blue.
We'll know every inch of this city,
From Balkaya to Kupuz,
The flower-filled gardens of the colliery,
The coal-moving wagons at port,
The pasty-faced people spilling
Onto the streets after work.

....

"Black, Zonguldak's black river runs
With coal, not shame, but dirty it runs,
And so pours the money, and so money comes."

Boats at harbour waiting to go,
Each to its distant horizon.

1945

Yenisi

The new one

(1947)

Souvenir

The knife wound on my brow
Was because of you,
My cigarette case is a keepsake.
"Drop everything and come"
Your telegraph reads.
How could I ever forget you,
Sweetheart, with your hooker's license?

July, 1940

[*Küllük*, 1.9.1940]

My gold tooth

Come, my lovely, sit beside me,
Let me buy you silk stockings,
Let me put you in cabs,
Let me take you to clubs.
Come,
Come my gold-toothed one,
My dolled-up, perfumed whore,
My high-heeled bebop girl, come.

Something fishy

Is the sea this beautiful everyday?
Does the sky always look this way?
Is it always this lovely,
This furniture, this window?
It's not,
By god it's not;
There's something fishy about it.

Poem with a club

One glass comes, another goes,
Finger-food of every kind.
One girlfriend sings in the club
Another sits beside me.
She drinks and drinks, the other gets jealous.
Don't be jealous, sugar, don't.
You have your place
And she has hers.

In

We have our sun-wrapped seas
We have our leaf-wrapped trees;
Day and night we come and go
Between our trees and seas
In poverty.

Poem with tweezers

Not the atom bomb,
Not the London Peace Conference,
In one hand tweezers,
A mirror in the other:
She couldn't care less!

Poem with a dove

I'd not heard a sound
Of pigeons and doves at the window.
Had that urge to travel
Stirred again in me?
What of that seaweed smell,
The screech of seagulls in the air.
What is it?
A journey, of course, a journey.

[*Varlık*, 1.1.1947]

Oh! My long lost youth!

Where was this melancholy then,
Crying so much,
Drifting off into song,
Partying seven days a week,
Today music, tomorrow a film,
The Family Garden café, you hating it,
You should have gone to the park,
My girl, known to everyone,
My girl,
Who I'm crazy about,
Hanging on her every word,
We made a palace of a hayloft.
Where,
Where,
Where was this melancholy then!

[1.2.1947]

For those who long for the sea

Boats pass in my dreams,
Multi-coloured boats, above rooftops.
Poor me,
Years longing for the sea,
"I gaze, gaze and weep."

I remember my first sight of the world
Through the opening of a mussel shell,
Green of sea, blue of sky,
The undulating lumpfish…
Salt still flows in my blood
Where the oyster shell cut.

What mad entry was ours
In snow-white spume and open sea,
Foam without grievance,
Foam in the form of lips,
Foam whose faithlessness
With men is faultless.

Boats pass in my dreams,
Multi-coloured boats, above rooftops.
Poor me,
Years longing for the sea.

[*Aile*, April 1947]

The Covered Bazaar

You know how unused laundry smells
In wooden closets.
Your shop smells that way too.
You didn't know my sister,
She'd have been a bride, had she not died.
These threads are her threads,
This bridal veil, her veil.
And these women in the window?
This one in blue,
This one in a green dress…
Do they pass the night standing like this?
And this pink cloth?
Doesn't it also have a story?
It's not called the Covered Bazaar for nothing;
The Covered Bazaar,
The covered box.

[*Varlık*, 1.3.1947]

Near death

Wintertime, early evening,
A sick man is at his window.
I'm not the only one alone.
The sea is dark, the sky too,
And the birds are unsettled.

I'm poor and alone but forget it
– wintertime, early evening comes –
I can count my share of lovers too.
I hungered for fame, women and money
But with time you work it out.

Do we grieve because we'll die?
What did we do or see
In this world apart from sin?

Death will clean us of dirt
In death we become good men.
We'll forget our thirst
For women, money and fame.

Poem with bells

We're civil servants,
At nine, at twelve, at five,
We're huddled on the street.
So the Almighty wrote our fate.
We either wait for the finish bell
Or for payday.

[*Varlık*, 1.12.1946]

Poem with a flutter

I woke and saw one morning
The sun had struck my heart,
I was like the birds and leaves
Fluttering in a spring wind.
I was like the birds and leaves,
My whole body's in revolt,
I was like the birds and leaves,
Birds
And leaves.

Sprawled out

Sprawled out, she lies full-length,
Her robe slightly open,
Her arm raised, armpit showing,
And with one hand holding her breast.
There's nothing in it, I know.
It's nothing to me either, but...
Then again
How can you lie like this!

[*Varlık*, 1.9.1946]

Altındağ

On the other side of Ankara there is a large and destitute district called Altındağ. The fragments you are about to read come from a larger poem about that part of town. As dawn approaches, the whole of Altındağ has a dream. Here you'll read only the dream of a young girl and a sewer worker.

One sees a husband in her dream:
A gentleman with a hundred-lira salary.
They marry and move to the city.
Letters are delivered to their address:
Happy Home apartments, basement flat.
They live in a flat the size of a box.
She cleans neither laundry nor windows
And if she washes pots, well they're her own.
They have a child, lit by a halo.
They buy a second-hand pushchair.
In the mornings they go to Kızılay Park
So that little Yılmaz can play in the sand,
Just like those well-mannered kids.

The sewer worker dreams of the bathhouse,
Sweetest of dreams.
He stretches out on the marble slab,
Attendants come and wait beside him.
One pours water,
Another rubs soap,
Another waits to towel him down.
As new customers arrive
The sewer worker
Goes out as clean as cotton.

Karşı

Up against it

(1949)

Days

There are days, I gather myself and leave,
In the smell of nets freshly hauled from the sea
Taking flight on the path of gulls
Drifting from one island to another.

There are unimaginable worlds,
Flowers open, erupt in noise,
Smoke bursts noisily from the earth.

But the seagulls, the seagulls,
Each feather bristling with haste!

There are days, blue all over me.
There are days, sunlight all over me.
There are days, delirious days…

[*Aile*, July 1947]

For you

For you, my fellow humans,
Everything is for you.
Night, and the day too, are for you.
Daylight and at night moonlight
Leaves in moonlight,
Wonder in leaves,
Wisdom in leaves,
A thousand greens in daylight,
Yellows are for you, pinks too.
Your touch of someone's skin,
Its warmth,
Its smoothness,
The comfort when lying down,
Greetings are for you
Swaying masts in the harbour are for you,
The names of days,
The names of months,
The paint on boats is for you,
The postman's feet,
The potter's hands,
Sweat dripping from brows,
Bullets fired in combat,
Graves are for you and gravestones,
Prisons, handcuffs, death sentences
For you.
Everything is for you.

[*Yaprak*, 1.5.1949]

I'm listening to Istanbul

I'm listening to Istanbul, my eyes closed.
First a gentle breeze
Slowly swaying
Leaves on the trees,
Far off, very far off
The water seller's unceasing bells.
I'm listening to Istanbul, my eyes closed.

I'm listening to Istanbul, my eyes closed.
Birds are passing by,
High up, in flocks, screeching,
Nets are being drawn from fish traps,
A woman dips her feet in water.
I'm listening to Istanbul, my eyes closed.

I'm listening to Istanbul, my eyes closed.
The cool air of the Grand Bazaar,
The bustle of Mahmutpaşa,
Courtyards full of pigeons,
Hammer blows from dockyards,
Smell of sweat in a sweet summer breeze.
I'm listening to Istanbul, my eyes closed.

I'm listening to Istanbul, my eyes closed.
Recalling drunken nights of old,
A shore-side mansion's disused boathouse,
Wrapped in the whir of a southern wind.
I'm listening to Istanbul, my eyes closed.

I'm listening to Istanbul, my eyes closed.
A pretty girl walks down the street,
There are curses, songs, ballads, catcalls,
There's something falling from her hand,

It must be a rose.
I'm listening to Istanbul, my eyes closed.

I'm listening to Istanbul, my eyes closed.
A bird flutters around your skirt,
I know, if your brow is hot or not,
I know, if your lips are moist or not.
A pale moon rises from behind the trees,
I can feel it in the beat of your heart.
I'm listening to Istanbul.

[*Varlık*, 1.6.1947]

Toward freedom

Before the sun is up,
When the sea is still brilliant white, you'll set off.
The pull of oars in your palms,
And the joy of work in your heart,
You'll set out.
On the swell and roll of nets, you'll set out.
Fish will meet you and mark your course,
And you'll be overjoyed.
When they shake the nets
Sea will come to your hands, scale by scale,
When the seagulls' souls are stilled
In their rocky graves,
Suddenly
New hope will break out on the horizon.
Mermaids and flocks of birds,
Or carnivals, parades, or festivals?
Wedding dances and circus acts or fairground rides?
Heeey!
What are you waiting for, throw yourself overboard,
Forget who's waiting for you on shore.
Can't you see, freedom is everywhere.
Be the sail, the oar, the rudder, the fish, the sea.
Go wherever you can.

[*Aile*, October 1947]

Galata Bridge

Planted on Galata Bridge
I happily watch you all.
Some are pulling on oars,
Some scrape mussels off pontoons,
Some hold the rudders of barges,
Some are coiling ropes,
Some are birds, flying, like poems,
Some are fish, glittering,
Some are ferries, some are buoys,
Some are clouds up high,
Some are tugs with funnels down
To quickly pass beneath the Bridge,
Some are horns sounding out,
Some are smoke pouring out,
But all of them are you, you…
Busy with the pull and thrust of life.
Am I the only hedonist here?
What the hell, maybe one day
I'll write a poem about you,
Earn a few coins for it
And fill my belly too.

[*Varlık*, 1.5.1947]

Up against it

Stretch, my body, stretch,
Face the rising day.
Let them feel if you can
Your powerful hands, your arms
Against the tide of public taste.

Look! The world, a riot of colour!
Be happy if you can
In this beautiful world
Despite the sickened multitudes.

Toiling endlessly away,
The cogwheel grinds,
And in among its teeth
The weak against the strong.
Everyone opposes something.
The little madam in her bed, asleep,
Wrestles with her dreams.

Stretch, my body, stretch,
Face the rising day.

[*Aile*, October 1949]

Mahmut the dreamweaver

This is what I do,
Every morning I paint the sky
While you are all asleep.
You wake and it's all blue.

Sometimes the sea is torn apart.
You've no idea who sews it up.
I do.

Sometimes I daydream too,
That's also my job.
I dream of a head within my head,
I dream of a belly within my belly,
I dream of a foot within my foot.
I don't know what else to do.

[*Yaprak*, 1.3.1949]

The first days of Spring

I'm lighter than a feather on mornings like these,
A patch of sun on the opposite roof,
The whistling of birds and songs in me,
I step out in full voice,
My head dizzy with Spring air.

I guess the days will always be this good,
Spring like this every morning,
Not a thought or care in the world.
"To hell with worry" I tell myself,
I'm happy being a poet,
It's enough.

[*Yaprak*, 15.5.1949]

Poem of loneliness

They've no idea, those who don't live alone,
How silence imparts fear
How people talk to themselves,
How they run to mirrors
Longing for a living soul,
They've no idea.

[*Meydan*, 15.5.1948]

Separation

Behind the departing boat, I stand, gazing;
I can't throw myself into the sea, the world's beautiful;
After all, I'm a man, I can't cry.

[*Aile*, October 1949]

Inside

Windows — the window's the best.
You can stare at passing birds at least,
Instead of the four walls.

[*Yaprak*, 1.6.1949]

See what happens

See what happens when you don't hear
The pistachio splitting apart on the branch,
Just see what happens to you.
See what happens, if you don't hear this rain
Or the tolling bell or the man talking,
See what happens if you don't smell the seaweed
Or the lobster, the shrimp,
Blowing in wind from the sea…

[*Yaprak*, 15.6.1949]

For free

We're living for free, for free;
Air is free, clouds are free
Valleys and hills are free;
Rain and mud are for free;
Car bodies
Cinema doors
Display windows are free;
Not so for bread and cheese
But saltwater's free;
Freedom costs you your head;
Slavery is free;
We're living for free, for free.

[*Yaprak*, 15.4.1949]

For the motherland

What didn't we do for this motherland!
Some of us died;
Some gave speeches.

[*Varlık*, 1.8.1946]

The Ahmets

Who, the man Ahmet
Who, the gentle Ahmet,
With the gentleman Ahmet,
The gentle gentleman Ahmet?

[*Yaprak*, 15.3.1949]

Poem on the attitude of Erol Güney's cat to Spring and social unrest

A tomcat and a piece of liver,
It's all she wants from life.
Great!

Poem on the pregnancy of Erol Güney's cat

Sneak out into the street on a spring day,
And that's what you get.
So there you stew
In your own thoughts.

Flea verse

A mess too difficult to comprehend!
All day, all night, without end.
To everyone we spill our heavy woes
But no-one asks us how it goes.

Some caught within their daily farce,
Some without pants upon their arse.
All have mouths and ears and noses,
Each deformed in different poses.

Some believe the words of prophets,
Some wear watches in their pockets.
Some write all that's thought or said,
Some are bums and have to beg.

Some bare arms with dedication,
Some observe the earth's rotation.
Some splash out and drink their fill
And in the morning pay their bill.

Is this the way it's got to be
An elephant eaten by a flea
When seven people in a house
Carve up and share a tiny mouse?

This mess, when all is said and done,
Is just a riddle, word-spun.
It's pointless asking what it means—
You'll find more gold in a hill of beans.

[*Varlık*, 1.7.1946]

Part Two

Toplanmayan şiirleri

Uncollected Poems

Poems published
1937—1950

Tree [i]

I threw a shoe at the tree,
My shoe never fell,
My shoe never fell,
The tree ate my shoe;
I want my shoe,
I want my shoe!

August, 1937

[*Varlık*, 15.9.1937]

---

[i] First published in *Garip* as 'Veda Müsameresi' and jointly attributed to Oktay Rifat and Orhan Veli.

Hoy lu-lu

I want to have black friends
With strange unheard-of names.
I want to sail with them
From the port of Madagascar to China.
I want one of them
To sing "Hoy lu-lu" to the stars
Each night on deck.

And one day suddenly
In Paris
To bump into one of them.

Ankara, August 1937

[*Varlık*, 15.9.1937]

Sea

In my room beside the sea,
I know without looking from the window
The boats going by outside
Are loaded up with watermelons.

The sea, just as I once did,
Likes to irritate me
By holding its mirror
To the ceiling of my room.

The smell of seaweed
And the net-poles dragged ashore
Mean nothing
To the children living on the coast.

Ankara, September 1937

[*Varlık*, 15.9.1937]

Slope

Evenings in the other world,
When factory shifts end,
If the road taking us home
Isn't this steep
Death won't be so bad.

Ankara, August 1937

[*Varlık*, 15.9.1937]

Journey

I've no plan to travel.
But if I had
I'd come to Istanbul.
What would you do
When you saw me on the Bebek tram?

Anyway, like I said
I've no plan to travel!

Ankara, August 1937

[*Varlık*, 15.9.1937]

Sunday evenings

I'm unkempt now, but
Once I've paid my debts
I'll probably have a new suit
And you probably
Still won't love me.
Then, passing through your neighbourhood
Done up in my Sunday best,
Do you think I'll hold you
As dear as I do now?

August 1937

[*Varlık*, 15.09.1937]

Poems on asphalt

I

What a great thing:
To see an unknown horizon
When a roadside building
Is pulled down.

II

I envy those kids
Lining up on the curb
Watching the steamroller
Rolling on.

III

Its sound
Reminds my friend
Of motorboats
Passing on the sea.

IV

I wonder
If it's only poets
Who stare at broken cobbles
And dream of gleaming asphalt?

Ankara, September 1937

[*Varlık*, 15.10.1937]

Edith Almera

Maybe right now he's
Thinking of Edith
Almera by a lake-
Side near Brussels.

Edith Almera
Darling of the nightclub scene
First fiddle
In a gypsy quartet.

Smiles
As she waves
To her clapping fans.

Nightclubs are beautiful;
A man
Might fall in love
With girls who play fiddle there.

Ankara, September 1937

(*Varlık*, 15.10.1937)

My tree

In our neighbourhood
If there'd been another tree but you
I wouldn't have loved you so.
But if you'd known
How to play hopscotch with us
I'd have loved you more.

Beautiful tree!
By the time you die
We'll have moved
God willing
To another neighbourhood.

Ankara, September 1937

[*Varlık*, 1.11.1937]

Being miserable

I might have been angry
With the people I love,
If love
Hadn't taught me
To be miserable.

Ankara, September 1937

[*Varlık*, 1.11.1937]

Bar

Since I don't love her now,
Why pass by the bar
Where I drank
And thought of her
Every night.

Ankara, September 1937

[*Varlık*, 1.11.1937]

Voyage

Willows are beautiful
But when our train
Makes its final stop
I prefer
To be a river
Than a willow tree.

On the train, October 1937

[*Varlık*, 1.11.1937]

People

II

Not always but especially
When I realize
You don't love me
I want to see you
As I saw other people
From my mother's lap
When I was young…

Ankara, September 1937

[*Varlık*, 1.11.1937]

Poems on travel

I

When you travel
Stars talk
And what they say
Is usually
Sad.

II

The melody you whistle
Is sweet
Those nights you're drunk.
But the same tune
At a train window
Isn't sweet at all.

On the train, October 1937

[*Varlık*, 15.12.1937]

Are you alive?

Trying to stick the tail
On the Devil's kite we made together,
I saw your little heart thumping.
I never once thought
To tell you what I felt.

I wonder if you're still alive?

Ankara, August 1937

[*Varlık*, 15.12.1937]

Morning

My hand like a many-branching tree
I grasp the sky
And gaze up at the clouds
As a camel runs and runs, running
To reach the far horizon
Before dawn...

Ankara, October 1937

[*Varlık*, 15.12.1937]

Suicide

No one must hear of it;
In the corner of my mouth
Will be a drop of blood.
Those who don't know me
Will say, "surely he loved someone".
Those who do will say,
"Miserable sod, he suffered a lot…"
But the real reason
Will be neither of these.

Ankara, December 1937

[*Varlık*, 15.12.1937]

Goldfinch

Pretty girl, but not
As sweet as the finch
Strutting over birdlime
I set on the plum tree's
Highest branch in the garden
When I was young .

Ankara, September 1937

[*Varlık*, 15.12.1937]

Letters to Oktay

I

                    10.12.37
                    Ankara
                    21:00

Winter, hellish…
My first letter
I write from the Hungarian Café.
Dear Oktay,
Tonight
All the drunks
Send greetings to you.

II

                    12.12.37
                    Ankara
                    14:30

Just now, it's raining outdoors.
Clouds pass through mirrors
And these days Melih and I
Are in love with the same girl.

III

                    06.01.38
                    Ankara
                    10:00

More than a month looking for work.
Penniless, in rags.
If I didn't love her
Maybe I wouldn't wait
For the day I die for others.

[*Varlık*, 15.1.1938]

Sabri the mechanic

Talking with Sabri
Always at night
And always in the street
And always drunk.
He always says,
"I'm late for home"
And always under his arm
Two loaves of bread.

October, 1937

[*Varlık*, 15.1.1938]

The Sicilian fisherman

A hundred years from now
When not a single man from our time
Is still alive, a fisherman
Living on the Sicily coast
Casting his nets on a summer morning
Will look at the sky, more open than usual,
And hum a line from my poems
And yet he will never know
A poet called Orhan Veli
Passed through this world…

I'm sure this beautiful thought
Will never come to pass
But for some reason
It seems very strange to me.

Ankara, August 1937

[*Gençlik*, 15.5.1937]

For something to do

All the beautiful women thought
Every love poem I wrote
I wrote for them.
But I always felt bad
Knowing I wrote them
Just for something to do.

Istanbul, November 1937

[*İnsan*, 1.10.1938]

My bed

Since I always think of her
In my bed at night,
While I love her still
I'll love my bed too.

30 January 1938

[*İnsan*, 1.10.1938]

The story of Ali Riza and Ahmet

How strange the story of Ali Riza
And Ahmet!
One lives in the village,
One in the city
And every morning
The city dweller goes to the village,
The villager to the city.

1938

[*İnsan*, 1.10.1938]

Barbecue

Some evenings the barbecue would burn at their door,
In the darkness nothing could be seen
Except for flame and smoke.
In lean years the plentiful coals
Brought peace and joy to the infant soul
Of my poet friend Oktay Rifat,
And his mother, Münevver Hanım,
Would grill fish on the barbecue
And with a cardboard fan my friend
Would fill his nostrils with its smoke.

1938

[*İnsan*, 1.10.1938]

My chatter

I was born in 1914,
Talked in '15,
I'm still talking now.
What happened to my chatter?
Did it reach the sky?
Maybe it will all return
In 1939
In the form of an aircraft.

If there is a God
I want nothing else from Him.
And what's more I don't want
His existence
Or *my* business
To be left to *Him*.

September 1939

[*Varlık*, 15.10.1939]

Like us

I wonder if a tank
Has desire in its dreams
And what does a plane
Think when it's alone?

Do gas masks hate to sing
In chorus, I wonder,
In moonlight?

And are rifles as merciless
As we humans?

September 1939

[*Varlık*, 15.10.1939]

Carnation

You're right, the death of ten
Thousand people in Warsaw
Probably isn't as fine as
The art of rhetoric, and
A detachment of troops
Is nothing like a carnation
"pursed from a lover's lips."

September 1939

[*Varlık*, 15.10.1939]

Bird and cloud [ii]

Birdman!
We have our bird,
Our tree too.
Give us just a penny's
Worth of cloud.

[*Varlık*, 15.3.1940]

[ii] Jointly attributed to Oktay Rifat and Orhan Veli.

Quantitative

I love beautiful women,
I love working women too;
Beautiful working women
I love more.

Ankara, January 1938

[*Varlık*, 15.3.1940]

Walking the streets

Walking the streets, when I catch
Myself smiling to myself
And think how crazy they'll suppose I am
I smile even more.

[*Varlık*, 15.3.1940]

I'm Orhan Veli

I'm Orhan Veli,
Who wrote the famous line
"It's a pity about Süleyman Efendi."
I hear you're curious
About my private life.
Then let me explain.
First I'm a man, that's to say
I'm not some kind of circus animal.
I have a nose, ears,
But not all that shapely.

I live at home
And I have a desk job.
I came into the world
With a mother and father.
My head isn't in the clouds,
And I'm not a paragon of virtue.
I'm not as modest
As the King of England
Nor as aristocratic
A Celâl Bey's stable boy.
I love spinach
And die
For puff pastry.
I don't give a shit for wealth.
By God, I don't!

I beat the streets
Without a bodyguard.
Oktay Rifat and Melih Cevdet
Are my best friends.
I have a girlfriend, respectable,
But I can't tell you her name.
Let the literary historians find her.

I busy myself with pointless things too
But the only "pointless" thing I don't do
is busy myself with rotten poets.

Then again
Maybe I have a thousand other habits.
But what's the point
In listing them all?
They're all the same.

April 1940

[*İnkılâpçı Gençlik*, 15.8.1942]

Hay Kay

Seaweed smell
And a plate of prawns,
At Sandıkburnu

[*İnkılapçı Gençlik*, 17.10.1942]

The water carrier's song

I carry water, my donkey leading.
Git, donkey, git!
I add life to a thousand lives each day.
Git, donkey, git!

Two flagons one side,
Two flagons on the other.
Sloshing, sloshing.
To a thousand lives each day I add life.
Git, donkey, git!

All I have in this world:
My wife, my donkey, my son.
Git, donkey, git!
May God grant you long life.
What will I do if you die?
Git, donkey, git!

The water he carries is butter to me, honey,
And milk to my wife.
Muddy water tastes just fine.
Everyday a hundred homes, a thousand heads.
Git, donkey, git!
Giver of life,
Giver of health,
Giver of plenty.

[*Yaprak*, 1.11.1949]

Wave

I

I want neither paper nor pen
To feel that I'm blessed
A cigarette between my fingers,
I dive down into the blue
Of the picture in front of me.

I go and the sea pulls me,
Sea pulls me and the world holds tight.
Is it something in the air
That drives you mad, makes you drunk?

I know, it's a lie, all lies;
That I'm a boat or a barge, it's a lie,
The water's coolness on my ribs,
Wind whistling through tie-lines,
The unceasing sound of a motor,
All lies.

But then,
Then there are beautiful days I transcend,
I transcend this blue wonder,
Like the melon rind floating in water,
The tree's silhouette struck against the sky,
The dew enveloping plums each morning,
The mist, the fog, the light, the scent…

II

Neither paper nor pen is enough
For me to feel that I'm blessed.
All of this... it's all rubbish.
I'm neither boat nor barge,
I should be somewhere else,
I *should* be somewhere else,
Not melon rind
Nor light, dew or fog,
But like a human.

[*Yaprak*, 1.12.1949]

Poem with a tail

We tread separate paths,
You're a butcher's cat, I'm a street cat,
You eat from a Kitty-Kat tin,
I pick scraps from a lion's jaw,
You dream of love, I dream of fish bones.

But your life isn't easy either, brother,
Not easy at all,
Having to shake that tail day and night.

[*Yaprak*, 15.12.1949]

Reply

– What the fat cat said to the alley cat –

You talk about hunger,
So you're a communist.
Then it was you who burnt all the buildings,
Those in Istanbul,
Those in Ankara…
What a swine you are!

[*Yaprak*, 15.1.1950]

Relief

You say I wish the struggle were over,
That I'd never be hungry,
Or tired.
You say I wish I never needed to piss,
Or sleep.

Then why not say I wish I were dead!

[*Yaprak*, 1.2.1950]

Adventure

I was small, so very small,
I cast my line in the sea,
Fish gathered in shoals,
I saw the sea.

I made a kite, nicely done,
It's tail the colour of a rainbow,
I raised it into the sky
And I saw the sky.

I grew up, jobless, half-starved,
I had to earn money.
I entered the thronging multitudes,
And that's when I saw people.

I'll turn my back on nothing,
Not my girl or my dreams,
Nor the sea or the sky…
And when I look at last
I'll still need to earn a living.

There you are, poor poets,
I say, that's all you'll see.

[*Yaprak*, 15.3.1950]

Suddenly

Everything happened so suddenly.
Shafts of daylight suddenly struck the earth,
The sky was suddenly there,
Suddenly blue.
Everything happened so suddenly,
Smoke suddenly started rising from the earth,
Shoots, suddenly, and buds,
Suddenly there was fruit.

Suddenly,
Suddenly,
Everything happened so suddenly.
Suddenly boys and girls,
Roads, meadows, cats and people…
Suddenly there was love,
Suddenly joy.

[*Yaprak*, 1.4.1950]

Mermaid

Perhaps she'd only just come from the sea,
Her hair, her lips
Held the scent of the sea until morning,
Her breasts rose and fell like the sea.

She was poor, I know
– But you can't go on forever about poverty –
She sang her song of love
Softly into my ear.

Who knows what she'd seen or learnt
In her intimate life with the sea!
Mending nets, casting them, hauling them out,
Setting rods, cutting bait, cleaning the boat…
She stroked my hands
And brought to mind the spiny fish.

I saw that night, saw it in her eyes
How beautifully dawn broke on the open sea!
Her hair taught me about waves,
And I went on swaying in dreams.

1943

[*Yaprak*, 15.6.1950]

Published Posthumously
1951–1967

Incoming poem

Quince, pomegranate from Istanbul it comes,
I turn around, a head-spinning beauty comes.
My money's a starvation wage,
But the creditors slip through.
Dear god,
I can't take it,
It's unbearable.

[*Varlık*, 1.1.1951]

Parade of love

That slender, stick-like girl was first,
Now a merchant's wife I suppose.
Who knows how fat she's grown.
But I'd still like to see her very much.
First love is never easy.

The second was Münevver, older than me,
Who doubled up laughing as she read
The letters I wrote and tossed into her garden.
I'm ashamed to remember those letters,
As if I'd just written then today.

....
...................we stopped in the street
.... so
.........written side by side on the wall
.... in fires.

The fourth was depraved,
She'd tell me everything—I mean *everything*,
She once stripped naked in front of me
And for years I couldn't forget it,
So often she came back in my dreams.

Let's skip the fifth and come to the sixth.
Her name was Nurinnisa.
Oh my beauty
Oh my brunette
Oh
My darling Nurinnisa.

Seventh was Aliye, a society girl.
But I never got used to her.

Like all society girls
It was all about earrings and furs.

The eighth was the same old shit.
You want virtue from another's wife
But asked of you, you throw a fit.
Anyway…
Lies are as cheap as chips.

Ayten was the name of the ninth.
At work she was everyone's slave
But when she left the bar
She slept with whoever she liked.

The tenth was smart
……………. left ……
But not without cause.
Making love is for the privileged few,
The rich or the unemployed.
When two hearts are intertwined
Nothing will keep them apart,
But two naked bodies, wow,
Look better in a bathtub.

The eleventh was a workaholic.
But what else could she be
Working all day for a despot.
……………………… Alexandra
At night she'd come to my room
And stay until morning.
She drank cognac, got drunk,
The next day she was at work by dawn.

Let's come to the last.
I've never been attached to anyone
As much as I was to her.
Not only a woman, but an individual.

Not mindlessly polite,
Nor obsessed with goods.
If we are free, she'd say,
If we are equal, she'd say.
She knew how to love people
As much as she loved living.

[*Son Yaprak*, 1.2.1951]

Poem with a hole

Pocket with a hole, jacket with a hole
Sleeves with a hole, caftan with a hole
Undies with a hole, shirt with a hole

Is the (w)hole of mankind a colander?

[*Yeni Dergi*, 1.3.1951]

Rubaiyat

Take a look at the secret of life
The tree with a single root left in soil
The world is so sweet that thousands
Go on living without arms or legs.

[*Aile*, April 1951]

To Live

I

I know, it's not easy to live,
To fall in love and sing to the one you love,
To stroll in starlight at night,
To warm yourself by the light of day,
To find time like this to meet
On Çamlıca Hill for half a day
– A thousand blues flowing from the Bosphorus –
To forget everything in these leagues of blue.

II

I know, it isn't easy to live,
But there
A dead man's bed is still warm,
Someone's watch still ticks on his wrist.
Living isn't easy, brothers,
But neither is dying.

It isn't easy to leave this world.

[*Aile*, April 1951]

My beloved

My sweetheart won't come to Claridge's
She'd never be seen in M&S

[*Yeni Dergi*, 1.2.1951]

Something like whisky

There's something like whisky in the air
Makes you feel down, down…
If you burn with longing, missing her
When your girl is somewhere else
And you're here
It makes you feel rough, rough…

There's something like whisky in the air
It makes a man drunk, drunk.

[*Varlık*, 1.9.1951]

Over it all

Birds pass over the cloud,
And rain pours over it.

Birds pass over a train,
And rain pours over it.

Birds pass over night,
And rain pours over it.

Moon comes, wherever birds go...
And sun rises over the rain.

March 1939

[*Vatan*, 16.11.1952]

Outside the city

Buds about to burst
Signal days of beauty
And a woman, outside the city,
On grass
Under the sun
Lying face down,
With the feel of spring
In her breasts and belly.

May 1939

[*Vatan*, 16.11.1952]

That's life

This house had a dog, curly
Called Dingdong — who curled up and died.
There was a cat too: Bluey,
She disappeared.
The daughter got married,
The son finished school.
All these bittersweet things
Happened in a year!
They all just happened like that…
That's life.

June 1939

[*Vatan*, 16.11.1952]

Renaissance

Tomorrow I should go to the wharf,
The Renaissance will arrive by ferry.
Let's see, what is the Renaissance?
How does it present itself?
Fashionable or a little tatty?
A politician, stick in hand?
Or whiskered, with a moustache,
Looking like a magician?
Will he spring from the cargo or the cabin?
Or some kind of stoker or other
Who'll work his passage here?

July 1939

[*Vatan*, 16.11.1952]

Butter

Uncle Hitler!
Come over and see us.
I'll show my mother
Your sideburns and whiskers
And in return I'll steal butter
From the kitchen cupboard
And give it to you.
You can feed it to your troops.

September 1939

[*Vatan*, 16.11.1952]

Gangster

(Hitler gives himself to literature)

All these years writing poems,
For what?
I'll be a bandit.

Let every highwayman know
There'll be no more work
For them when I'm here.

Since I'm stealing food
From their hands,
Let them in turn take my place.

There's an empty seat at the writing desk.

September 1939

[*Vatan*, 16.11.1952]

Goodbye

My road is asphalt,
My road is earth,
My road is sky,
My road is the public square
And what am I thinking!

Love, rain,
Sound of a tram,
The hotelier…
And I mumble a line
Warm as a pleasing meal.

*

Postman, cop and unemployed
Still they come and go.
Only Niyazi
The late Süleyman Efendi's son
Sits in the coffeehouse.
He listens to news and thinks:
"Will there be war?
Will there be famine?"

Or maybe he already knows
He'll soon be going to war.

October 1939

[*Vatan*, 16.11.1952]

Recreation

Why are there lights in this mountain house
At such an hour after midnight?
What are they doing inside?
Talking or playing some kind of game?
Maybe this, maybe that…

If talk, what are they talking about?
About the war, or about taxes?
Maybe they're doing nothing at all.
The children are sleeping,
The father is reading a paper,
The mother is sewing.
But maybe they're really doing nothing.
Who knows,
Maybe there are no words
For what they're doing.

February 1940

[*Vatan*, 16.11.1952]

On mustard

What an idiot I was,
For years I never understood
The social rank of mustard.
Abidin often said this in the past:
"You can't live without mustard."
To those closer
To higher truths,
I know, it's not an absolute must,
But may God not deprive them of mustard.

March 1940

[*Vatan*, 16.11.1952]

Lady in a white cloak

From Kalender she boarded the boat
Lady in a white cloak.
In one hand an umbrella,
With the other she opens her fan.
On Friday she goes to Göksü
Lady in a white cloak

September 1940

[*Vatan*, 16.11.1952]

Yob

You twag off school,
Catch birds,
Go down to the sea
And gab with yobs
You scrawl graffiti on walls;
It's nothing much,
You'll turn my head too.
What a yob you are!

April 1941

[*Vatan*, 16.11.1952]

Thank God

Thank God, there's someone else in the house,
There's a breath,
There are footsteps;
Thank God, thank God.

[*Yeni Ufuklar*, May 1959]

Flag

On a battlefield
Palms filled with my blood,
Head under my torso
Leg slung over my arm,
My lifeless, prostrate brother!
I know neither your name
Nor your crime.
Maybe we're on the same side,
Maybe we're enemies.
Perhaps you know me.
I'm the one who sings in Istanbul,
The one gunned down over Hamburg,
The one wounded on the Maginot Line,
The one who starved to death in Athens
The one taken prisoner in Singapore.
I didn't script my own fate.
But I know all this as much
As the one who wrote that script,
The taste of strawberry ice-cream,
The joy in the sound of a jazz band,
The roller-coaster ride of fame.
I know you like the finer things too,
Apart from tea and simits,
And a scruffy old overcoat,
Like artichoke dressing, creamed foul,
A tumbler
Of Black & White whiskey,
Garments of ermine and fur.
Twenty years of strife
Weighed against a single bullet;
Fated
To start life in Kharkov;
Forget it.

We brought a flag this far,
Others will carry it further;
In this vast world
There are two million of us,
And well we know ourselves.

[*Papirüs*, 1.1.1967]

Masterpiece

It's not my habit
To write poems when I'm in love.
But I wrote my real masterpiece
When I realized
It was her I loved the most.

So it'll be to her
I read this poem first.

Ankara, September 1937

[*Papirüs*, 1.6.1967]

Bebek suite

In eight parts.

Road

The road is straight.
The tram passes over it,
Men pass,
Women pass.

Women

Women…
Morning and night
Waiting for the tram
In front of Regie's.

Green

The colour they like
Is green.
Food baskets
In their hands.

Driver

Always looks ahead,
Doesn't smoke.
He's an eccentric guy
This driver.

Landscape

Houses, shops, walls:
Coal depots,
Sea;
Skiffs, barges, triremes.

Sea

Who doesn't love the sea
Once you've stood
On its shore
And pulled in a fish.

Fishermen

Our fishermen
Don't sing
Like those in books
From the same song sheet.

Your house

You can travel
All these roads by tram.
But your house
Is the furthest.

Istanbul, October 1937

[*Papirüs*, 1.6.1967]

To leave a city

This is the city for walking in the rain
Staring at quayside barges
Humming a tune at night.
This city is full of streets,
And through them thousands come and go.

And even though she's a White Russian
The waitress who brings me tea each night,
Who I'm fond of too, is in this city.

The old pianist, who winks at me when he turns
From time to time from his waltzes
And foxtrots to sneak in snatches of Brahms
And Schumann, he's in this city too.

The ferries carrying passengers to the village
Where I was born are in this city.
My memories are in this city.
Those I love,
The graves of those dead.

This city is where I work,
Where I earn my bread.
And despite all this,
Still this is the city I'm leaving
Because of a woman
In another city.

Istanbul, 18 November 1937

[*Papirüs*, 1.6.1967]

A tiny heart

(*After Jules Supervielle*)

Along the asphalt
A girl passes with a bike
Between her legs
A fluttering pigeon
And a tiny heart…
A tiny heart pulsing.

[*Papirüs*, 1.6.1967]

Landscape

The moon rose over the opposite house.
Evening coolness spread out.
There are sounds of trams,
The smell of the sea from far away.
I'm so moved by this landscape.

April 1940

[*Papirüs*, 1.6.1967]

Pictures

None of them belong to her,
Yet all these paintings
Have sad names:
"April Morning",
"After Rain"
And "The Dancer"
Looking at them
Makes me want to cry.

April 1940

[*Papirüs*, 1.6.1967]

Notes

Orhan Veli's poems are filled with geographical locations: names of cities, towns, and villages, streets, cafés, restaurants, and bars. These notes attempt to clarify some of the more obscure cultural references and allusions.

Hakan Sazyek's *Cumhuriyet Dönemi Türk Şiirinde Garip Hareketi* (Akçağ Yayınları, 2006) is a useful guide to the *Garip* poets in general, and I have consulted it several times in compiling these notes.

The information in square brackets beneath many of the translations indicates the place and date of first publication in the original Turkish.

'NEARING GEMLIK'
Gemlik : Known as Kios until 1922, Gemlik is situated on the Sea of Marmara, approximately 18 miles from the city of Bursa.

ROBINSON CRUSOE
One of the earliest Turkish translations of Jonathan Swift's *Gulliver's Travels* (1726) was by Mahmud Nedim in 1872, under the title *Güliver Nam Müellifin Seyahatnamesi* (1872). The first Turkish translation to be published in the Latin script was *Cüceler ve Devler Memleketinde Gulliver'in Seyahatleri* (1935) by Ercümend Ekrem. It is just as likely that Veli read the story in translation from English to French.

PUBLIC HOLIDAY
'When the cannon goes off...' : In many Turkish cities during the month of Ramazan the firing of a cannon signals the end of the day's fast. Though the cannon on the last day of Ramazan brings the fasting period to an end, Eid al Fitr, the Feast of the Breaking of the Fast, Şeker Bayramı or the Sugar Festival in Turkey, begins the following day on the first of Shawwal. Veli is a little quick off the blocks.

Ministry of War : Veli gives its Ottoman title, *Harbiye Nezareti*, which was situated in a magnificent building in the Fatih district of Istanbul, occupied by Istanbul University since 1933. Veli studied in the Philosophy department from 1933 to 1936.

GOSSIP
Yuksek Kaldirim: A street in the Beyoğlu district of Istanbul. Famous for its many steps, it was once the main thoroughfare leading from Galata Tower to the Golden Horn. One of the oldest booksellers in Istanbul, Librairie de Pera, is located here.

"Your pain is in my heart": Alludes to the popular song, in the Turkish classical tradition (Türk Sanat Müziği), composed by Saadettin Kaynak (1895-1961) to lyrics by Ali Vecdi Bingöl (1888-1973). Zeki Müren's timeless version on *Saadettin Kaynak Sarkıları* (Kalan CD, 2005) is readily available online.

EPITAPH
Part I of 'Kitabe-i Seng-i Mezar' sparked a long-running public debate about the moral and aesthetic value of Veli's "new" poetry. In particular, the controversy centred on Veli's closing line, 'Yazık oldu *Süleyman Efendi*'ye!', which many critics believed typified the brash, new anti-poetry of the *Garip* movement. It also gave rise to the first allegations of plagiarism against Veli where some critics perceived an uncomfortable degree of similarity between the closing line of 'Kitabe-i Seng-i Mezar' and Paul Verlaine's 'Priez pour le pauvre Gaspard'. Hakan Sazyek's study of the *Garip* movement, *Cumhuriyet Dönemi Türk Şiirinde Garip Hareketi* (2006) highlights compelling evidence of Veli's close reading of several French sources, such as Paul Eluard in his poem 'Dağ başı', here translated as 'In the Sticks'.

BEAUTIFUL WEATHER
Pious Foundations : From the earliest days of the Ottoman Empire, Islamic religious organisations often administered a portfolio of properties called *evfak*. These properties were either donated or appropriated on the organisation's behalf and put to charitable use. A centralized directorate of charitable endowments, the Evkaf Nazırlığı, was created in 1826. From the 1920s and throughout Veli's time to the present the vast revenue of rents paid for 'evfak' properties is administered by *T.C. Başbakanlık Vakıflar Genel Müdürlüğü*, The General Directorate of Charities of the Turkish Prime Ministry.

IT MAKES ME BLUE
Üsküdar: A district in Istanbul on the Asian shore of the Bosphorus.

HERO OF A NOVEL
Bay of Saros : Situated on the Aegean coast of the Gallipoli peninsula in north-western Turkey.

JOURNEY
Uzunköprü : Meaning literally *long* (uzun) *bridge* (köprü), Uzunköprü is the name of a district and a small town in Edirne Province, approximately 6 kms from the border with Greece. Situated on the banks of the river Ergene, the town was founded in 1444 as Cisr-i Ergene (The Ergene Bridge), changing its name to Uzunköprü in 1917. It was occupied by Greek forces from 1920 to 1922 during the Turkish War of Independence.

SONG OF ISTANBUL
Rumeli Hisar : Fortress built by Sultan Mehmet II between 1451 and 1452, located on the European shore of the Bosphorus, in what is now the Sarıyer district of Istanbul. Veli is buried a stone's throw from Rumeli Hisar in the Aşiyan Asri Cemetery.

KEŞAN
The title names both a district and a large town in Edirne Province.

SONGS OF THE ROAD
In Autumn 1945 Veli travelled from Istanbul to the Black Sea town of Zonguldak, a prominent coal mining centre. This poem, Veli's longest, makes frequently allusions to "Türkü" and "Mâni" folk songs and ballads, folk heroes and folk legends. The use of quotation marks indicates where these moments occur. Much of the poem relies on the fourteenth-century folk poet, Köroğlu, who lived in and around Bolu, and the long poem credited to him, *The Epic of Köroğlu*, about a legendary character reminiscent of Robin Hood. *Köroğlu* rebels against a local landlord, *Bolu Beyi* and kidnaps his daughter, *Döne*, who he marries. *Ayvaz* and *Hoylu* are characters in the story. *İsa Balı* is the name of a local village. There are also many place names, of villages and streets, in and around Zonguldak.

Ada : probably refers to Adapazarı, a city between Bolu and İzmit.

Regie : *Memalik-i Şahane Duhanları Müşterekül Menfaa Reji Şir-keti* or "Reji" for short, was a private tobacco and alcohol monopoly established in 1883. Veli refers to the company headquarters at No. 5 Mimar Vedat Sokak in Sirkeci. The restored building is now home to the Régie Ottoman Istanbul Hotel.

SOUVENIR
'...*lover's license*' : In Veli's poem the word 'vesika' refers to an official document or permit for a woman to work in a *pavyon* (a nightclub) or in a brothel. The person addressed here is either a *konsomantris*, a woman who drinks and chats with customers in a 'pavyon', or a prostitute. There is a wonderful film which borrows Veli's line for its title, *Vesikalı Yârim* (1968) directed by Ömer Lütfi Akad, staring Türkân Şoray and İzzet Günay.

POEM WITH TWEEZERS
London Peace Conference : Convened in December 1912. The Ottoman Empire withdrew following the 'Raid on the Sublime Porte' in 1913, a coup d'état led by Enver Pasha.

PEOPLE
Presumably, this is the second of a two-part sequence. Part I is missing.

LETTERS TO OKTAY
Addressed to his close friend and fellow poet Oktay Rifat (1914-1988).

'*Melih and I*' : Veli's friend, the poet Melih Cevdet Anday (1915-2002).

CARNATION
"...pursed from a lover's lips" : A quotation from the symbolist poet Ahmet Haşim (1885-1933). The original reads: "Yârin dudağından getirilmiş".

HAY KAY
Sandıkburnu : A famous and immensely popular up-market *meyhane* (restaurant bar) of the 1920s and 1930s in the Yenikapı district of Istanbul.

PARADE OF LOVE
The only surviving draft of this poem was found after Veli's death, wrapped around a toothbrush. See Nemet-Nejat, M. (1989) *I, Orhan Veli*. (New York, NY: Hanging Loose Press).

To Live
Çamlıca Hill : A popular picnic area in Veli's day, on the Asian side of Istanbul in Üsküdar.

That's life
In Turkish the dog is called 'Çinçon'. There really isn't a better translation than Talat Halman's 'Dingdong', which I freely borrow here. See 'Such is Life' p.135 in Halman, T.S. (1997) *Just for the Hell of It*. (Istanbul: Multilingual).

About the translator

George Messo spent more than a decade in Turkey, as a mountaineer, teacher, civil servant, and university lecturer. His poetry and translations have been widely published in Europe and the United States. His critical writing appears in *World Literature Today, Adirondack Review,* and *New York Quarterly*. He has published three collections of poetry with Shearsman, most recently *Violades & Appledown* (2012), as well as several translations. His anthology *İkinci Yeni: The Turkish Avant Garde* (Shearsman Books, 2009) was shortlisted for the European Poetry Translation Prize in 2010.

Messo divides his time between Turkey, Saudi Arabia, and northern Sweden, where he lives with his wife and children.

www.ingramcontent.com/pod-product-compliance
Lightning Source LLC
Chambersburg PA
CBHW022008160426
43197CB00007B/333